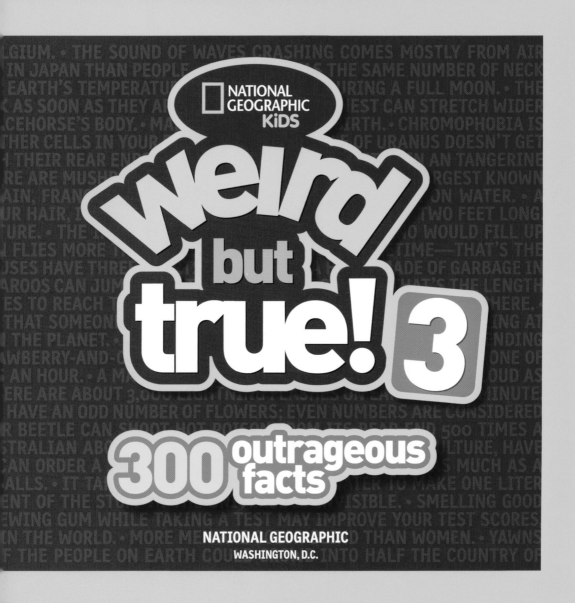

NATIONAL
GEOGRAPHIC
KiDS

weird
but
true! 3

300 outrageous facts

NATIONAL GEOGRAPHIC
WASHINGTON, D.C.

# BE A STAR!

*Weird but True 3!* is the first book in the *Weird but True* series to include **"FAN FACTS"**—totally outrageous facts submitted by kids. Like all of the facts in this book, FAN FACTS are 100% true. We know because we checked them with experts. You'll see these FAN FACTS sprinkled throughout the book along with the names of the fans who submitted them.

If you love *Weird but True*, go online for even more fun and information about the *Weird but True* book series. ngkidsweirdbuttrue.com

**4**

# Octopuses
## have
## three
## hearts.

THE UNIVERSE IS ABOUT 13.7 BILLION YEARS OLD.

KANGAROOS CAN JUMP MORE THAN 30 FEET (9 m) IN ONE HOP. THAT'S THE LENGTH OF 12 SKATEBOARDS!

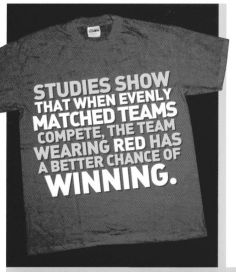

**STUDIES SHOW** THAT WHEN EVENLY **MATCHED TEAMS** COMPETE, THE TEAM WEARING RED HAS A BETTER CHANCE OF **WINNING.**

One of the shortest wars ever lasted 38 MINUTES.

There was a **hotel** made of **garbage** in Rome, Italy.

LEMONS CAN HAVE MORE SUGAR THAN STRAWBERRIES.

**The Earth spins so fast that someone standing at the Equator is traveling at about 1,000 miles an hour.**

(1,600 km/hr)

It would take a stack of more than 100,000 giraffes to reach the outermost layer of the Earth's atmosphere.

The Earth weighs about
6,600,000,000,000,000,000,000 metric tons.

(1 metric ton=2,204.6 pounds)

Legend says that Aztec ruler Moctezuma drank 50 cups of hot chocolate a day.

ELEPHANTS CAN RUN FASTER THAN HUMANS.

YOU LOSE UP TO 100 HAIRS A DAY.

A warm frog makes faster croaking noises **than a cold frog.**

THE FIRST AIRPLANE JOURNEY ACROSS THE UNITED STATES TOOK 49 DAYS.

SEEING THE COLOR RED CAN MAKE YOUR HEART BEAT FASTER.

SOME DIAMONDS ARE MORE THAN A BILLION YEARS OLD.

IT'S POSSIBLE TO PRODUCE ELECTRICITY FROM ELEPHANT DUNG.

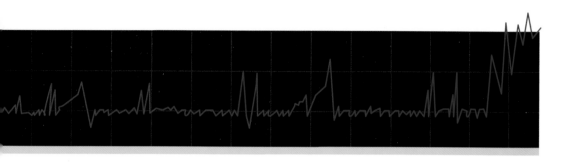

IF HUMANS CAME IN AS MANY SIZES AS DOGS, WE'D RANGE FROM **THREE** TO **EIGHTEEN** FEET TALL.

(91.4 cm to 5.5 m)

Some astronauts living on the *Mir* space station ate Jell-O every Sunday to help keep track of the days.

# AN AVERAGE MAJOR LEAGUE BASEBALL IS USED FOR ONLY SIX PITCHES.

YOUR FEET HAVE 500,000 SWEAT GLANDS.

SAUCER-SHAPED LENTICULAR CLOUDS HAVE BEEN MISTAKEN FOR UFOS.

ALL THE MINED GOLD IN THE WORLD CAN FILL TWO OLYMPIC-SIZE SWIMMING POOLS.

A **man** once ate **49** glazed doughnuts in **8 minutes.**

**More than a thousand Earths could fit inside Jupiter.**

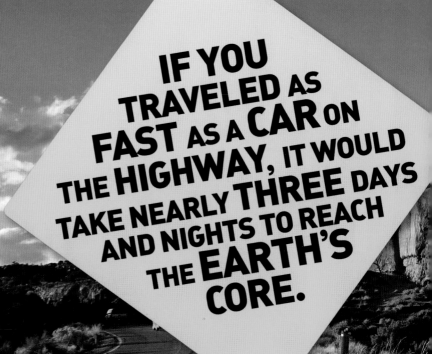

IF YOU TRAVELED AS FAST AS A CAR ON THE HIGHWAY, IT WOULD TAKE NEARLY THREE DAYS AND NIGHTS TO REACH THE EARTH'S CORE.

DAYS WERE ONLY 18 HOURS LONG A BILLION YEARS AGO.

THERE ARE **HUNDRED-FOOT-TALL** (30 m) SAND DUNES IN ALASKA.

A queen bee can lay **2,000** eggs a day in the spring.

SCORPIONS GLOW UNDER BLACK LIGHT.

A woman's **heart** usually beats faster than a man's **heart.**

It's impossible to see a full rainbow in the sky at noon.

Some **FROGS** survive the winter by freezing almost solid.

Four-thousand-year-old popcorn

was found
in a cave
in New Mexico, U.S.A.

# A lizard sticks its tongue out to smell.

FAN FACT! SUBMITTED BY BEN D., 9

In Italy, you can buy fresh pizza from a vending machine.

SATURN'S RINGS ARE MADE OF ICE AND ROCKS.

A gold-plated bicycle sold for £80,000 ($125,344) in the U.K.

Sperm whales have the heaviest BRAINS on the planet.

# A cat has about 20 muscles in each ear.

Certain sharks walk on their fins **underwater.**

# Some moths drink the tears of elephants.

In the summer, the amount of water pouring over Niagara Falls (on the U.S.-Canada border) each second could fill 13,000 bathtubs.

**Your brain** *is about three-quarters* **water.**

**Frog bones grow new rings as they age, just like trees.**

**Dirty snow** melts faster than **clean snow.**

Humans can make **10,000** different facial expressions.

THE OLDEST **ROCKS** IN THE **GRAND CANYON** ARE ALMOST **TWO BILLION** YEARS OLD.

Cheetah ancestors roamed North America about four million years ago.

Every zebra's stripe pattern is different.

THE **CORPSE FLOWER** GROWS UP TO **12 FEET TALL** (3.7 m) AND SMELLS LIKE **ROTTING MEAT.**

WHAT STINKS?

One of the world's fastest snakes—the **black mamba**—slithers up to **7** miles an hour. (11 km)

A MALE AFRICAN CICADA CAN MAKE A SOUND AS LOUD AS A POWER MOWER.

A RIPE CRANBERRY WILL **BOUNCE.**

You can buy a **cupcake-shaped designer handbag—** with strawberry-and-chocolate-colored crystals— for $4,295.

43

# TROPICAL
## RAIN FORESTS
### ARE A HABITAT FOR
## 80 PERCENT
### OF THE WORLD'S
## INSECT SPECIES.

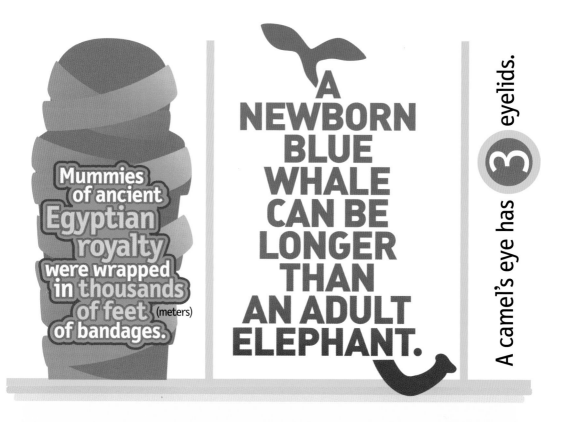

**Mummies of ancient Egyptian royalty were wrapped in thousands of feet (meters) of bandages.**

A NEWBORN BLUE WHALE CAN BE LONGER THAN AN ADULT ELEPHANT.

A camel's eye has **3** eyelids.

EVERY CONTINENT HAS A CITY **CALLED ROME** (EXCEPT ANTARCTICA).

# Newborn dolphins sleep for only a few seconds at a time.

**Earth's temperature rises slightly during a full moon.**

MOUNT EVEREST IS ABOUT **27** TIMES TALLER THAN THE EIFFEL TOWER.

**Yawns** are contagious for **chimpanzees,** just as they are for **humans.**

Every (6.5 sq. cm) square inch of your skin hosts about 6 million bacteria.

BUTTERFLIES MUST WARM THEIR WINGS IN THE SUN BEFORE FLYING.

**Guinea pigs** can walk as soon as they are born.

FAN FACT! SUBMITTED BY ALEC S., 11

**Your stomach would digest itself without mucus.**

The world's largest known **crystal** is **37.4** (11.4 m) feet long. That's 8 times taller than an average 10-year-old.

An eagle's nest can s t r e t c h wider than your sofa.

**HUMANS** have lived on Earth for about **200,000** years; **DINOSAURS** walked the planet for roughly *160 million years.*

MORE THAN

# 99PERCENT

OF THE SPECIES THAT
HAVE EVER EXISTED ARE NOW

EXTI

NCT.

**O**live **oil** and **garlic** are **real** ice-cream flavors.

FAN FACT! SUBMITTED BY CARSON B., 11

Some pet spas serve catnip tea to feline guests.

Catnip Blend

Spit can *freeze in midair* at the North Pole.

LAIKA THE DOG WAS THE FIRST "ASTRONAUT" TO TRAVEL INTO SPACE.

THERE ARE
ABOUT
3,000
LIGHTNING
FLASHES
ON
EARTH
EVERY MINUTE.

55

**SKUNKS HAVE STRIPED SKIN UNDER THEIR FUR.**

Blondes have more hairs on their heads than brunettes.

## THE BIGGEST KNOWN DINOSAUR SKULL

# THE FIRST SPACE TOURIST PAID $20 MILLION FOR A TEN-DAY TRIP TO THE INTERNATIONAL SPACE STATION.

**BOUQUETS** IN AUSTRIA HAVE AN ODD NUMBER OF **FLOWERS;** EVEN NUMBERS ARE CONSIDERED **BAD LUCK.**

## IS LONGER THAN A RACEHORSE'S BODY.

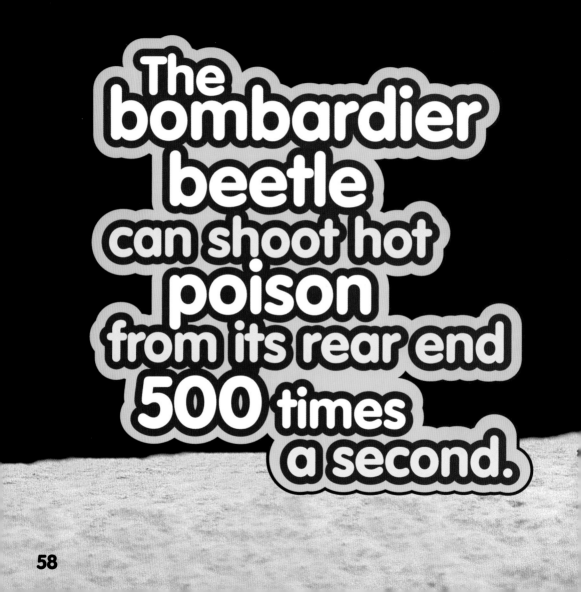

The **bombardier beetle** can shoot hot **poison** from its rear end **500** times a second.

# Some **sea stars** break off their own arms **when frightened.**

YIKES!

The largest known ant supercolony stretches nearly **4,000 miles** (6,440 km) **through Portugal, Spain, France, and Italy.**

The Hawaiian alphabet has only 13 letters.

YOU CAN BUY FAKE EYEBROWS AND EYELASHES MADE OUT OF REAL HAIR.

THE HARDER YOU CONCENTRATE, THE LESS YOU BLINK.

# Crocodiles
## sometimes
# walk on the backs of hippos.

# A river in Canada once turned red.

SHALOM HEI BAREV KUMUSTA SALAAM KIA ORA
APA KHABAR NI HAO HALLO ZDRAVO
BONJOUR GOEDENDAG HUJAMBO HEI SA'LAM
YIA SOU TIENA YISTILIGN MINGALA BA
MBOTE **Nearly** BOM DIA SOUR SDEY
AHOJ! **7,000** XIN CHÀO
BOK JÓ NAPOT
AHLAN WA SAHLAN
AKWAABA DIA DHUIT
MONI **languages** MALO
ANNYONG HASEYO SALEM
LABAS HOLA **are spoken** TERVIST
SABBAI DII SAIN BAINA UU
MERHABA **worldwide.** OI
VITAYU HALLÓ JAMA NGAA CZEŚĆ WHAH GWAAN
PRIVYET JAMBO KONNICHI WA HEJ
SAWATDEE NAMASTE BUNĂZIUA E KARO GRÜTSIE
CIÀO MHOROI MBA'ÉICHAPA ASSALAMO ALAIKUM

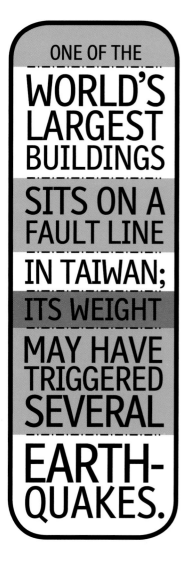

ONE OF THE WORLD'S LARGEST BUILDINGS SITS ON A FAULT LINE IN TAIWAN; ITS WEIGHT MAY HAVE TRIGGERED SEVERAL EARTH-QUAKES.

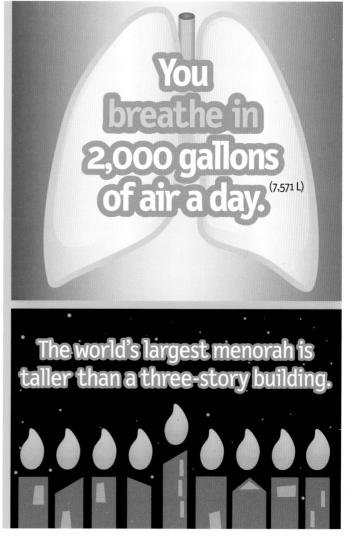

You breathe in 2,000 gallons of air a day. (7,571 L)

The world's largest menorah is taller than a three-story building.

# MALE WOODCHUCKS ARE CALLED HE-CHUCKS; FEMALES ARE CALLED SHE-CHUCKS.

The smallest **bone** in the **human body** is shorter than **a grain of rice.**

CAMELS CHEW IN A FIGURE-EIGHT MOTION.

The **oldest chocolate** ever found was inside a **2,600-year-old pot** in Belize.

STUDIES SHOW THAT **PAINTING YOUR ROOM BLUE** COULD MAKE YOU MORE CREATIVE.

A SHARK CAN LIVE FOR SIX WEEKS WITHOUT EATING.

# THE WORLD'S POPULATION GROWS BY ABOUT A BILLION PEOPLE EVERY 12 YEARS.

# Small icebergs
### are called
## growlers and
## bergy bits.

# There was once a lake the size of England in the Sahara.

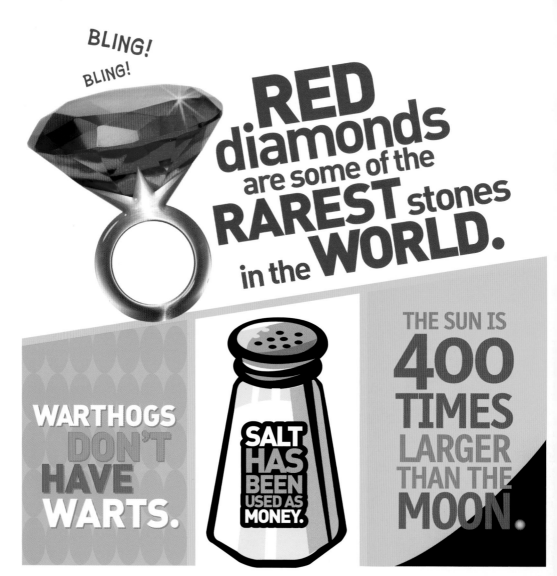

BLING!
BLING!

**RED** diamonds are some of the **RAREST** stones in the **WORLD.**

WARTHOGS DON'T HAVE WARTS.

SALT HAS BEEN USED AS MONEY.

THE SUN IS **400** TIMES LARGER THAN THE **MOON.**

A baby humpback whale drinks up to 130 gallons of milk each day.

(492 L)

got whale milk?

# Mantis shrimp can see colors better than humans can.

Australian Aborigines, the world's oldest living culture, have existed for at least 50,000 years.

**astro**
# h₂o

## Astronauts drink recycled urine.

**A METEORITE ONCE HIT A MAILBOX IN GEORGIA, U.S.A.**

Parrots talk without **vocal cords.**

# HAIR
### GROWS ALMOST EVERYWHERE ON YOUR
# SKIN
### EXCEPT YOUR LIPS, THE PALMS OF YOUR HANDS, AND THE SOLES OF YOUR FEET.

Months that begin on **SUNDAYS** always have a Friday the 13th.

Rats can't **burp.**

TEST FLIGHTS OF THE **FIRST SPACE SHUTTLE** TOOK OFF FROM THE BACK OF A FLYING **747.**

e=mc²

# Dolphins may be smarter

**than chimpanzees.**

# AN AUSTRALIAN MAN FOUND A 60-POUND (27-kg) GOLD NUGGET USING A METAL DETECTOR.

# Chromophobia is the extreme fear of colors.

No country owns **?** ANTARCTICA.

AT A RESTAURANT IN MICHIGAN, U.S.A., YOU CAN ORDER A **SUPERSIZE HAMBURGER** THAT WEIGHS AS MUCH AS A **GROWN MAN.**

Most spiders have **8** eyes.

Most swans in

The heaviest known hailstone weighed more than 7 baseballs.

England belong to the Queen.

Some
**CLOUDS**
are more than
**10 miles** (16 km)
**TALL.**

A beaver's home is called a lodge.

# SATURN HAS MORE THAN 60 MOONS.

It takes **three liters** of freshwater to make **one liter** of bottled water.

COULD YOU SPEAK UP?

**A praying mantis has only one ear.**

The north pole of **Uranus** gets no **sunlight** for about **42 years** at a time.

# ALL OF THE PEOPLE ON EARTH

# COULD CROWD INTO HALF
# THE COUNTRY OF BELGIUM.

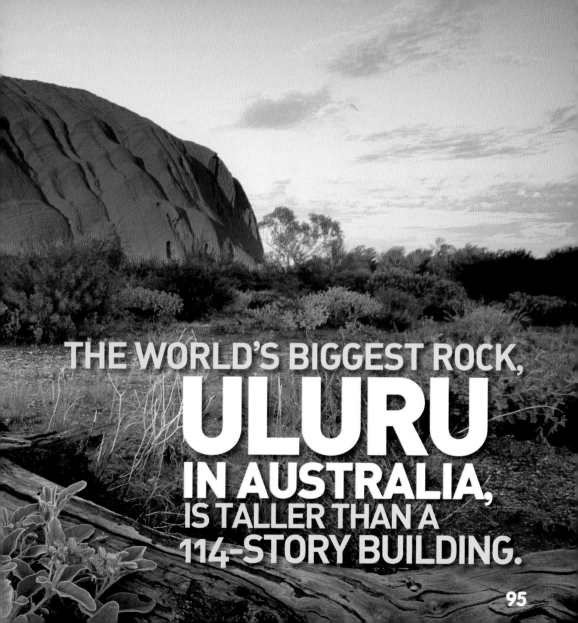

THE WORLD'S BIGGEST ROCK, **ULURU** IN AUSTRALIA, IS TALLER THAN A 114-STORY BUILDING.

A geep is part goat, part sheep.

96

There are more pets in

# Japan

than children.

SMELLING GOOD SCENTS, SUCH AS ROSES, WHEN YOU SLEEP MAY GIVE YOU HAPPY DREAMS.

A goldfish will turn gray if kept in the dark for a long time.

ANCIENT GREEKS USED hula hoops.

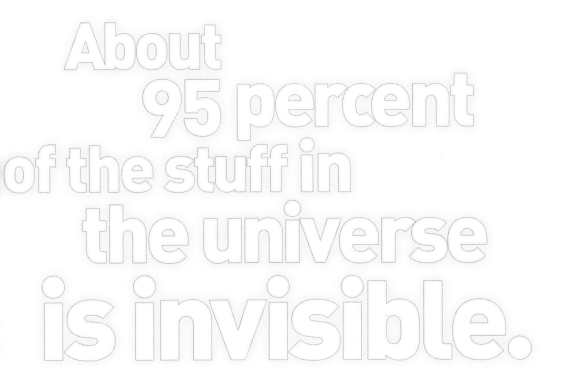

About 95 percent of the stuff in the universe is invisible.

# HORSES CAN TRAVEL UP TO (160 km) 100 MILES IN A DAY.

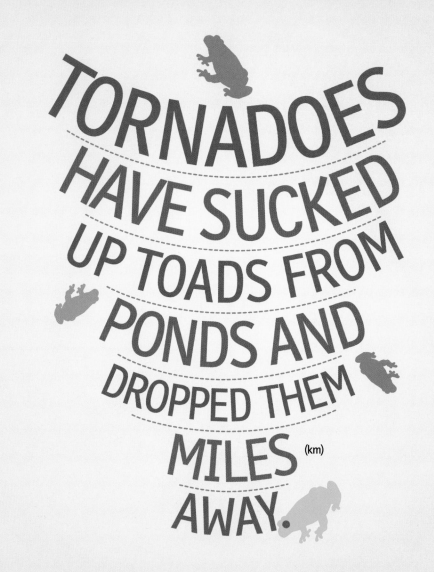

TORNADOES HAVE SUCKED UP TOADS FROM PONDS AND DROPPED THEM MILES (km) AWAY.

102

A group
of jellyfish
is called a
**smack.**

It would take more than 1,500 human hearts to equal the weight of a blue whale's heart.

**SOME GEESE CAN SOAR TO 32,000 FEET—**
(9,750 m)
**HIGH ENOUGH TO SEE A 747 PASSENGER JET FLY BY.**

The surface of the moon is smaller than Asia.

OUR UNIVERSE HAS NO CENTER.

FLAMINGOS' ANKLES LOOK LIKE KNEES.

The oldest
**koi fish**
lived to be

# 226
years old.

A **ROCK PYTHON** CAN LIVE FOR A YEAR WITHOUT A MEAL.

THERE ARE VOLCANOES INSIDE SOME GLACIERS.

It's impossible for turtles to stick out their tongues.

YOU CAN BUY SOAP THAT SMELLS LIKE BACON FRYING.

# A hamster's teeth never stop growing.

THE OLDEST KNOWN **PINE TREE** IS MORE THAN **4,700** YEARS OLD.

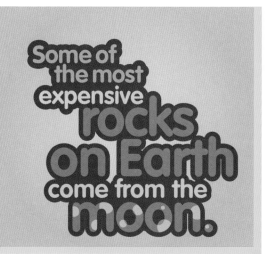

Some of the most expensive **rocks on Earth** come from the **moon.**

**A GIRAFFE HAS THE SAME NUMBER OF NECK BONES THAT YOU DO: SEVEN.**

Dogs pant up to 300 times a minute.

A group of rhinos
is called a
**crash.**

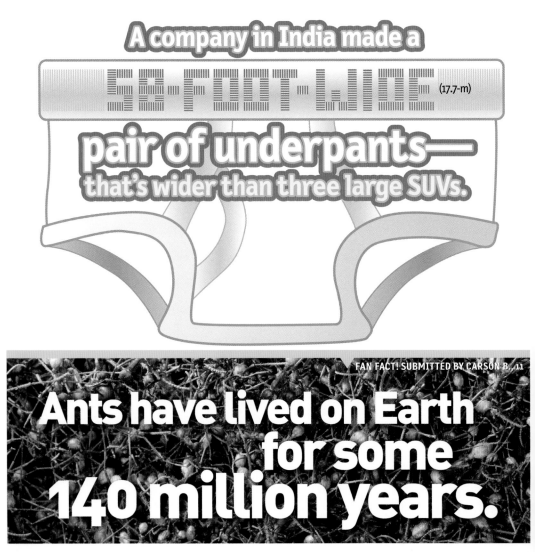

A company in India made a **58-FOOT-WIDE** (17.7-m) **pair of underpants—** that's wider than three large SUVs.

**Ants have lived on Earth for some 140 million years.**

A man in Canada can balance 17 spoons on his face at once.

A rooster is also called a **chanticleer.**

**CHEWING GUM** WHILE TAKING A TEST **MAY IMPROVE YOUR TEST SCORES,** ACCORDING TO ONE STUDY.

**A** canary **can sing two different songs** at the same time.

RAW TERMITES TASTE LIKE PINEAPPLE.

The scientific name for a gorilla is *Gorilla gorilla.*

The
star-nosed
mole
can find
and eat a
snack
in 230
milliseconds—
faster than
any other animal.

**Honeybees have hair on their eyeballs.**

YOUR SENSE OF **SMELL** IS WEAKER IN THE MORNING **AND STRONGER IN THE EVENING.**

**You can buy sneakers dipped in 18-karat gold for $4,053.**

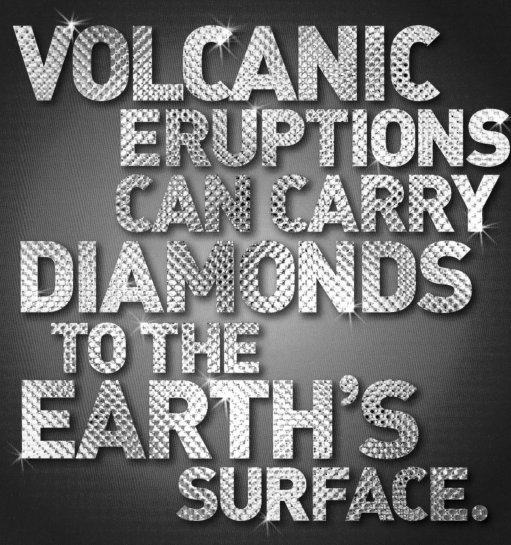

VOLCANIC ERUPTIONS CAN CARRY DIAMONDS TO THE EARTH'S SURFACE.

A man once made **956** pancakes in one hour.

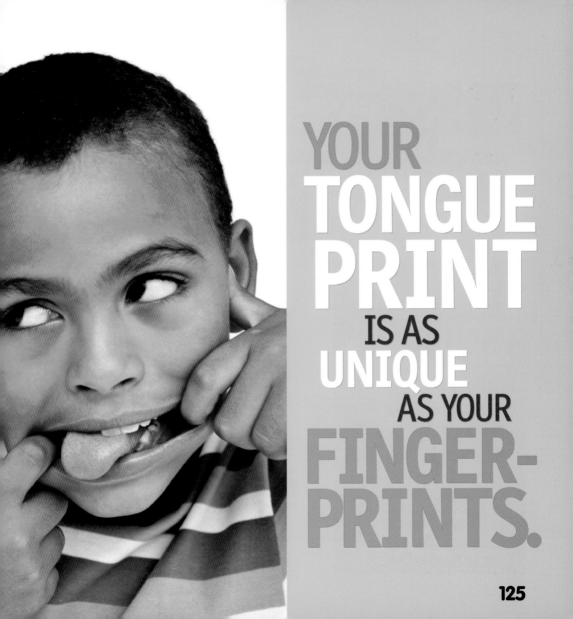

YOUR **TONGUE PRINT** IS AS **UNIQUE** AS YOUR FINGER- PRINTS.

**125**

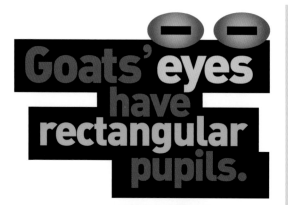

Goats' **eyes** have **rectangular** pupils.

**A British man ate 36** cockroaches **in 1 minute.**

SOME SPIDERS CATCH AND EAT FISH.

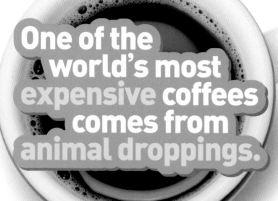

One of the world's most expensive coffees comes from animal droppings.

# Birds don't sweat.

FAN FACT! SUBMITTED BY SAMANTHA E., 11

# Wombat waste is cube-shaped.

**Paul** the octopus correctly predicted that Spain would win the 2010 World Cup.

A SALMON'S SENSE OF SMELL IS THOUSANDS OF TIMES BETTER THAN A DOG'S.

Baby **alligators** **bark** when they are ready to hatch **out of their eggs.**

A group of seagulls i.

# alled a squabble.

KIDS' FINGERPRINTS **DISAPPEAR** FROM SURFACES FASTER THAN ADULTS' DO.

Some parrots dance when they hear music.

**6009** is the next year that will look the same right side up and upside down; the last one was **1961**.

YOUR **TEETH** ARE HARDER THAN YOUR BONES.

An *inventor* *created a* *cell phone* *that recharges* *on* *Coca-Cola.*

A housefly can turn somersaults in the air.

An inventor created **edible** dinner plates.

A tightrope walker i.

A restaurant in Taiwan serves **food** in bowls shaped like **toilets.**

A 57-year-old ball of twine weighs **19,000** pounds— (8,618 kg) that's heavier than three hippopotamuses!

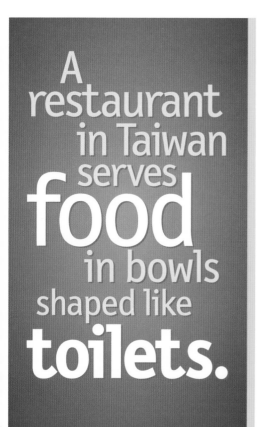

called a **funambulist.**

The
tallest wave
to reach land was
taller than the
Empire State
Building.

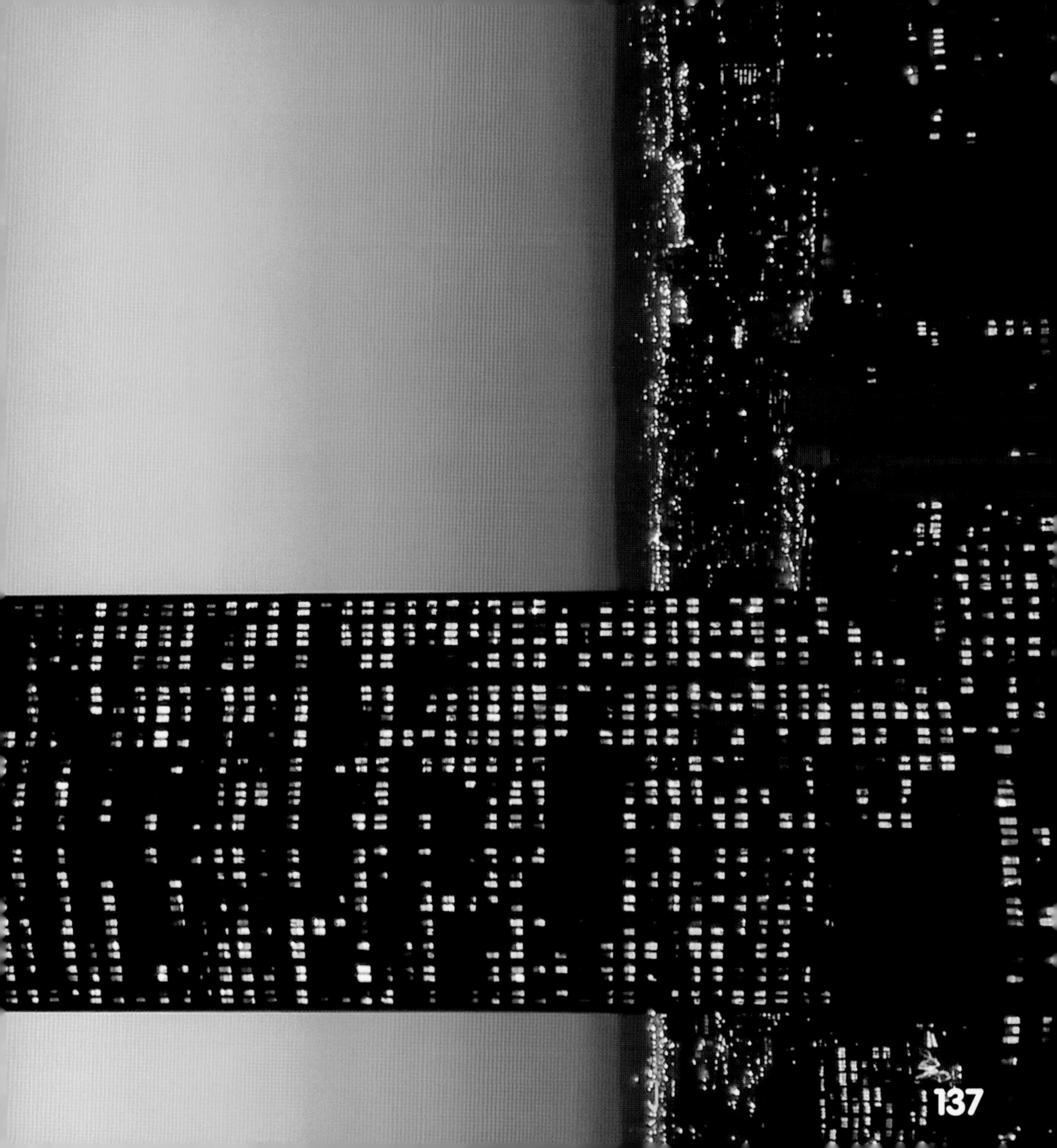

# HERRING COMMUNICATE BY PASSING GAS.

An **ortanique** is a cross between a **tangerine** and an **orange**.

300 MILLION YEARS AGO, SIX-FOOT-LO (1.8-m)

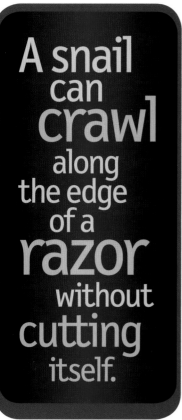

A snail can **crawl** along the edge of a **razor** without **cutting** itself.

# MOSQUITOES

PREFER TO BITE PEOPLE WITH

# SMELLY FEET.

FAN FACT! SUBMITTED BY LINDSEY Y., 11

ILLIPEDES ROAMED THE EARTH.

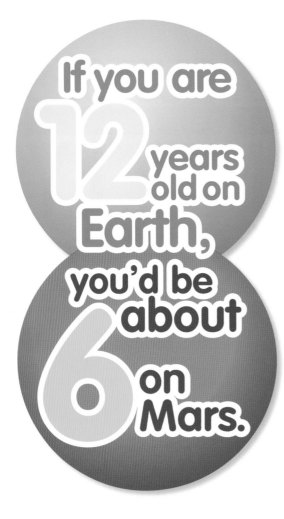

If you are **12** years old on Earth, you'd be about **6** on Mars.

Some **tree snakes glide** up to **78 feet** (24 ▶ through the air. THAT'S THE LENGTH OF TWO LARGE SCHOOL BUSES.

**Mexico City** has sunk **26 feet** (8 m) in the last **100 years.**

# You can buy an inflatable TV screen.

## The temperature on the moon can be hotter than boiling water.

A VOLCANIC ERUPTION in 1883 made the SUN LOOK GREEN.

THE
**DEAD
SEA**
IS SEVEN
**TIMES**
SALTIER
THAN THE
**OCEAN.**

Tiny bugs live in your eyebrows.

**FAN FACT!** SUBMITTED BY MARVIN P., 8

Saturn would float in water.

# Some pigs are afraid of mud.

# Male seahorses give birth.

# APPLES FLOAT BUT PEARS SINK.

More than **70%** of the **Earth's surface** **is water.**

**Early golf balls were stuffed with bird feathers.**

# LARGE FOREST FIRES CAN CREATE TORNADOES MADE OF FLAMES.

▲ **FAN FACT!** SUBMITTED BY JESSICA M., 9

A fifteen-year-old **cat** has probably spent **ten years** of its life **sleeping.**

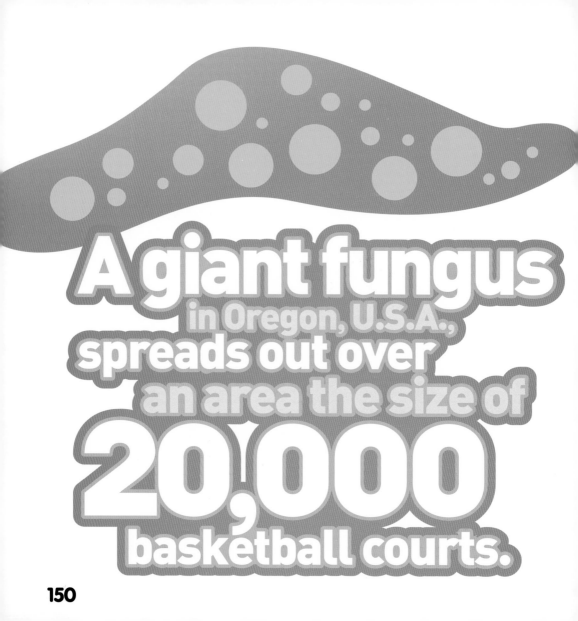

A giant fungus in Oregon, U.S.A., spreads out over an area the size of 20,000 basketball courts.

Some monkeys in Thailand teach their young to floss.

**FAN FACT!** SUBMITTED BY EMILY E., 11

## MALE PLATYPUSES CAN STING YOU WITH THEIR FEET.

THERE ARE SOLID GOLD, PIZZA-SIZE CANADIAN COINS WORTH **ONE MILLION** CANADIAN DOLLARS.

(US $1 million)

## LAWS IN ENGLAND

WERE WRITTEN **IN FRENCH** FOR MORE THAN **400 YEARS.**

**151**

# Bat hair
## HAS BEEN USED AS money.

**FAN FACT!** SUBMITTED BY TAYMAR W., 14

A Russian man drove a **tractor** more than **13,000 miles** (20,900 km) **in 19 days**— that's longer than the distance from London, England, to Los Angeles, California, U.S.A.

SOME VILLAGES IN POLAND HAVE MORE STORKS THAN PEOPLE.

A crocodile in **Australia** walked more than **250 miles** (400 km) to get back home.

BOY, MY FEET ARE TIRED.

ANTARCTICA

IS A DESERT.

A Finnish man wrote a novel

made up of

1,000 text messages.

You can shine your shoes with a banana peel.

AUSTRALIA'S **GREAT BARRIER REEF** CAN BE SEEN FROM SPACE.

Cold stars are red.

Hot stars are blue.

Some lizards can **walk** on water.

157

You can buy bat droppings for about $10 a pound.

Chewing gum while peeling onions may keep you from crying.

**The tallest** known living **man** is **8 feet,** (246 cm) **1 inch tall—**

a foot and a half (45.7 cm) **taller** than an average pro basketball player.

**IT TAKES 8 MINUTES AND 19 SECONDS FOR LIGHT TO TRAVEL FROM THE SUN TO EARTH.**

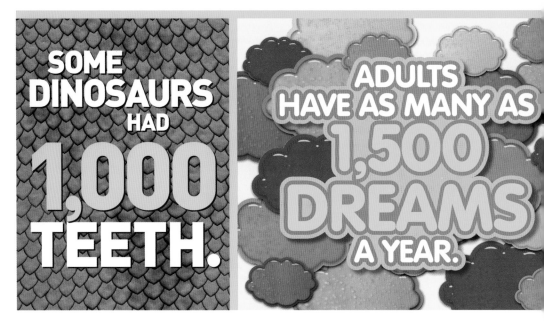

**SOME DINOSAURS HAD 1,000 TEETH.**

**ADULTS HAVE AS MANY AS 1,500 DREAMS A YEAR.**

**Bees** can be green, blue, or red.

**A farmer in Lebanon grew a 25-pound potato.** (11-kg) That's the weight of two bowling balls!

**FAN FACT!**
SUBMITTED BY CARLY L., 11

**163**

The world's largest **swimming pool,** in Chile, stretches **for half a mile.**
(0.8 km)

A
**flamingo**
can eat only
when its head
**is upside
down.**

A HOUND DOG NAMED TIGGER HAD EARS THAT WERE EACH

**14** INCHES LONG—

(35.6 cm)

THAT'S LONGER **THAN TWO OF THESE BOOKS** SIDE-BY-SIDE.

**Almonds** belong to **the rose family.**

You can get insurance that covers you in case of injury by a falling coconut.

FAN FACT! SUBMITTED BY MCKENZIE B., 12

# SOME MAKEUP HAS FISH SCALES IN IT.

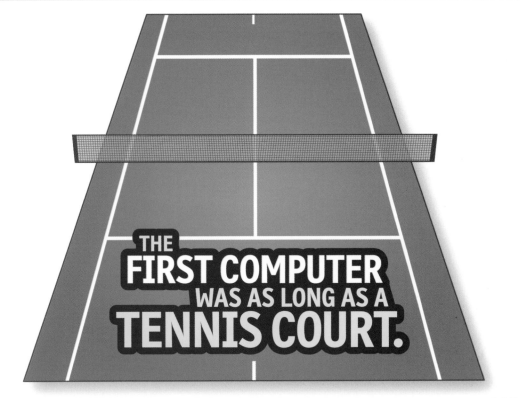

**BABIES' CRIES CAN SOUND DIFFERENT IN DIFFERENT LANGUAGES.**

THE **FIRST COMPUTER** WAS AS LONG AS A **TENNIS COURT.**

# The sound of waves crashing comes mostly from air bubbles.

A Scottish dish called haggis is cooked inside a sheep's stomach.

Rainbow-colored grasshoppers live in the rain forests of Peru.

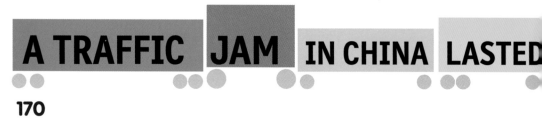

A TRAFFIC JAM IN CHINA LASTED

You can buy **worms** from a vending machine in Japan.

FOR MORE THAN A WEEK.

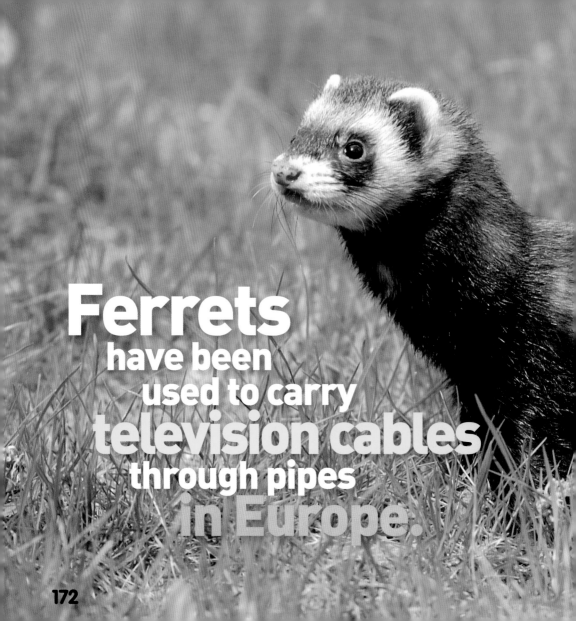

**Ferrets** have been used to carry **television cables** through pipes in Europe.

THE SHORTEST PROFESSIONAL BASEBALL PLAYER WAS 3 FEET, 7 INCHES (109 cm) TALL, THE HEIGHT OF AN AVERAGE 5-YEAR-OLD.

FAN FACT! SUBMITTED BY JACKSON G., 11

If you never **cut your hair**, it would likely stop growing at about **two feet long.** (61 cm)

SOME **BIRDS** CAN USE THEIR **BILLS** TO MEASURE THE TEMPERATURE OF THEIR **NESTS.**

A **MAN** DRESSED AS SANTA CLAUS WENT SKYDIVING OVER THE **NORTH** POLE.

Half the world's oxygen is made in the ocean.

YOU ARE MORE LIKELY TO BE IN A BAD MOOD ON THURSDAYS, ACCORDING TO A RECENT STUDY.

**Brain cells** live longer than all of the other cells in your body.

# A FIVE-SEAT BICYCLE IS CALLED A **QUINDEM**

# THERE ARE MORE SPECIES OF BEETLES ON EARTH THAN OF ANY OTHER CREATURE.

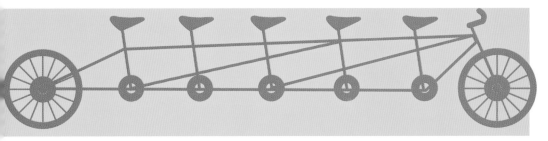

# A BUILDING IN POLAND LOOKS LIKE IT'S MELTING.

AN EARTHQUAKE **IN CHILE** SHORTENED THE LENGTH OF AN EARTH **DAY** BY 1.26 MICROSECONDS.

THE LENGTH of YOUR **FOOT** is about EQUAL to

the DISTANCE FROM your **ELBOW** to YOUR wrist.

There is no time at the center of a black hole.

LACHANOPHOBIA is the fear of vegetables.

# YOU CAN COMPETE IN AN underwater mountain bike race

## IN WALES, UNITED KINGDOM.

A sailfish can leap through the air at **68** miles an hour— (109 km/hr) that's about the speed a car drives on the highway.

# THERE ARE ABOUT 70 LAKES HIDDEN UNDER THE ANTARCTIC ICE.

Leeches can live in your nose.

Some baby birds use claws on their wings to climb trees.

There are mushrooms that glow in the dark.

PUG + BEAGLE

PUGGLE

**BARBIE'S PETS HAVE INCLUDED A LION, PARROT, AND GIRAFFE.**

Rotten eggs float in water.

You can write about 45,000 words with an average pencil.

Penguins swim up to **3,100 miles** in a year. (5,000 km)

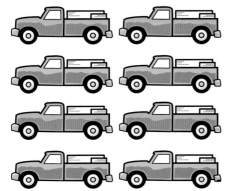

THE INFORMATION STORED ON AN **iPOD NANO** WOULD FILL UP **EIGHT PICKUP TRUCKLOADS** OF PAPER.

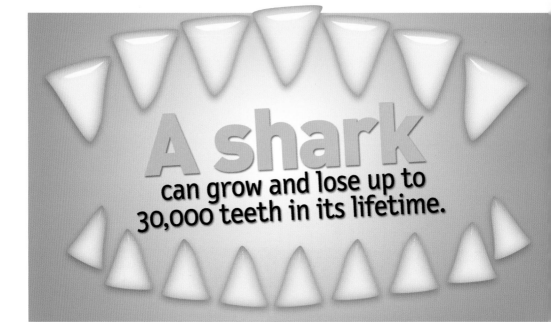

**A shark** can grow and lose up to 30,000 teeth in its lifetime.

**HARMLESS MICROSCOPIC SHRIMP** MAY LIVE IN YOUR DRINKING WATER.

**Some artists use chewing gum** to make paintings.

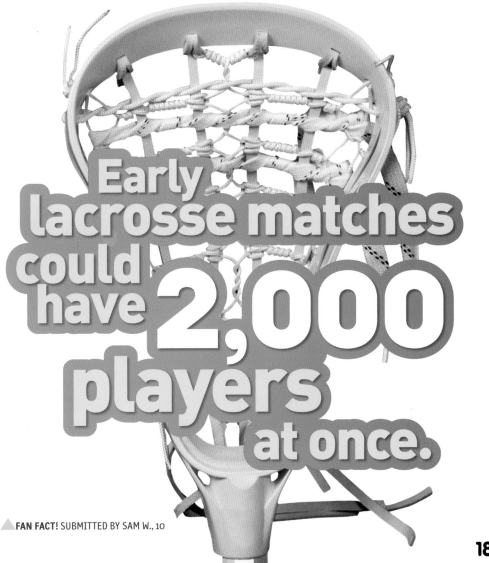

Early lacrosse matches could have **2,000** players at once.

# A British candy company created a giant box of chocolates filled with

## 220

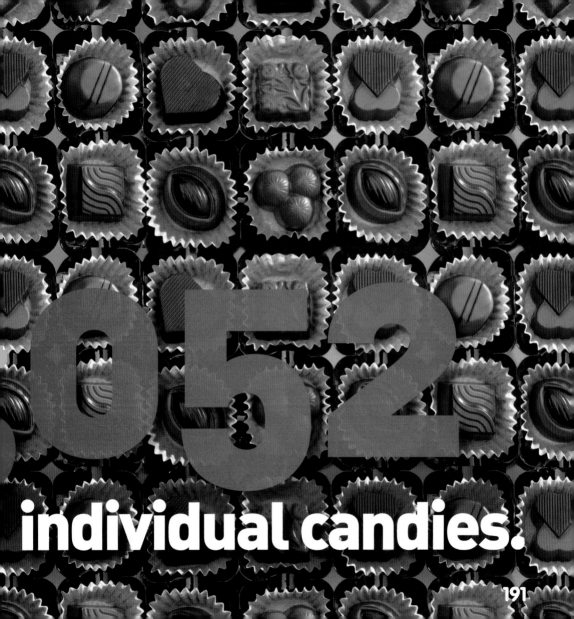

# 052

## individual candies.

There is a museum devoted to **ramen noodles** in Japan.

**FAN FACT!** SUBMITTED BY AIDAN C., 9

# SOME TURTLES BREATHE THROUGH THEIR REAR ENDS.

FAN FACT!
SUBMITTED BY
ANNA M., 8

Woodpeckers once **pecked holes** in the space shuttle.

# BALD EAGLES CAN SWIM.

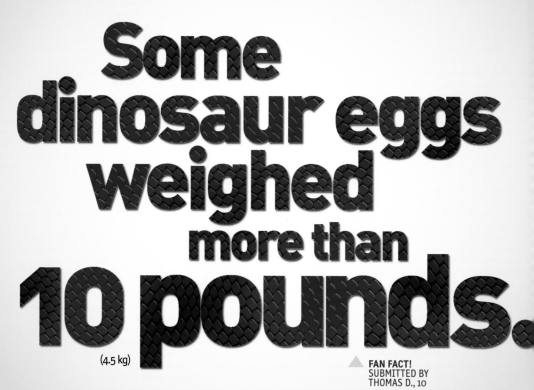

Some dinosaur eggs weighed more than 10 pounds.

(4.5 kg)

FAN FACT!
SUBMITTED BY
THOMAS D., 10

**A BIRD CALLED THE ARCTIC TERN FLIES MORE THAN A MILLION MILES** (1.6 million km) **IN ITS LIFETIME—**

THAT'S THE SAME DISTANCE AS MAKING THREE ROUND-TRIP FLIGHTS TO THE MOON.

▲ **FAN FACT!** SUBMITTED BY ZAID A., 11

Circus workers call the toilet a doniker.

It takes **713 GALLONS OF WATER** (2,700 L) to make one cotton T-shirt.

ZOOKEEPERS
ARE BITTEN

MORE OFTEN
BY ZEBRAS
THAN BY
TIGERS.

▲ FAN FACT! SUBMITTED BY **RORY AND KIERNAN F.,** 10

**197**

A Chinese man can **blow up balloons** using his **ears.**

It's not
possible
to
TICKLE
yourself.

# FACTFINDER

Illustrations are indicated by **boldface.**

**201**

Since 1888, the National Geographic Society has funded more than 12,000 research, exploration, and preservation projects around the world. The Society receives funds from National Geographic Partners, LLC, funded in part by your purchase. A portion of the proceeds from this book supports this vital work. To learn more, visit www.natgeo.com/info.

For more information, visit www.nationalgeographic.com, call 1-800-647-5463, or write to the following address:
National Geographic Partners, LLC
1145 17th Street NW
Washington, D.C. 20036-4688 U.S.A.

**Staff for This Book**
Robin Terry, *Project Editor*
Eva Absher, *Art Director*
Rachael Hamm Plett, *Designer*
Kathryn Robbins, *Design Production Assistant*
Lori Epstein, *Senior Illustrations Editor*
Michelle Harris, *Researcher*
Kate Olesin, *Editorial Assistant*
Hillary Moloney, *Illustrations Assistant*
Janice Gilman, *Illustrations Intern*
Grace Hill, *Associate Managing Editor*
Lewis R. Bassford, *Production Manager*
Susan Borke, *Legal and Business Affairs*

**Based on the "Weird But True" department in *National Geographic Kids* magazine**
Julide Dengel, *Designer*
Robin Terry, *Senior Editor*
Jay Sumner, *Photo Editor*
Marilyn Terrell, Jeffrey Wandel, Erin Whitmer, *Contributors*

**Manufacturing and Quality Management**
Christopher A. Liedel, *Chief Financial Officer*
Phillip L. Schlosser, *Senior Vice President*
Chris Brown, *Technical Director*
Rachel Faulise, *Manufacturing Manager*
Nicole Elliott, *Manufacturing Manager*
Robert Barr, *Manufacturing Manager*

Visit us online:
Kids: kids.nationalgeographic.com
Parents: nationalgeographic.com
Teachers: nationalgeographic.com/education
Librarians: ngchildrensbooks.org

For information about special discounts for bulk purchases, please contact National Geographic Books Special Sales: ngspecsales@ngs.org

For rights or permissions inquiries, please contact National Geographic Books Subsidiary Rights: ngbookrights@ngs.org

NATIONAL GEOGRAPHIC and Yellow Border Design are trademarks of the National Geographic Society, used under license.

Library of Congress Cataloging-in-Publication Data

Weird but true 3!: 300 outrageous facts.
    p. cm.
Includes index.
ISBN 978-1-4263-0766-9 (pbk. : alk. paper)
1. Curiosities and wonders--Juvenile literature. I. National Geographic Society (U.S.)

AG243.W383 2011
031.02--dc22

                                        2010037904

Printed in China
16/PPS/4-BX

WEIrDEsT, SMELLIEST, FASTEST, SLOWEST, BIGGEST, TINIEST, LOUDEST, DEADLIEST

NUMBERS come ALIVE in this action-packed book, filled with mind-blowing animal stats, species smackdowns, cool lists, plus fun and games.

NATIONAL GEOGRAPHIC KiDS

ANIMAL RECORDS

THE BIGGEST, FASTEST, GROSSEST, TINIEST, SLOWEST, AND SMELLIEST CREATURES ON THE PLANET

KATHY FURGANG AND SARAH WASSNER

IN OUR WORLD

OCTOPUSES: BIG BRAINS AND BIG SMARTS

OCTOPUSES HAVE THREE HEARTS

So you read on page 25 that octopuses are supersmart, but did you know that scientists study their brains to learn more about yours? Proportionate to size, octopuses have the largest and most complex brains of all invertebrates. Their brains are very different from ours, yet octopuses display some of the same smarts. They recognize their own names, solve puzzles, and pry open childproof jars. By studying octopus brains, researchers think they can learn about how our own noggins store and recall information. They also hope to figure out how the eight-armed egg-heads display humanlike actions while having such a unique nervous system. And perhaps they might even discover ways that human intelligence could evolve.

AN OCTOPUS BRAIN HAS ABOUT 300 MILLION NEURONS (NERVE CELLS)

33

# weird but true! 3

**Did you know that you have the same number of**

# neck bones as a giraffe,

**that Mount Everest is**

# 27 times taller than

**the Eiffel Tower, or**

**that rats can't burp?**

The creators of **NATIONAL GEOGRAPHIC KIDS,** the nation's most popular kids' magazine, bring you even more of this best-selling series for fact-lovers everywhere!

300 more wacky facts!

**Brain-tickling trivia** about animals, outer space, crazy inventions, the human body, weather, food, geography, and more!

Packed with fun photos and illustrations on every page!

**kids.nationalgeographic.com**

$7.95 U.S./$8.95 CAN/£5.99 UK

ISBN 978-1-4263-0766-9 /Printed in China

50795

9 781426 307669